A GREAT GAME!

The Sims

BY MARI BOLTE

NorwoodHouse Press

Norwood House Press

For information regarding Norwood House Press, please visit our website at www.norwoodhousepress.com or call 866-565-2900.

Credits
Editor: Kristy Stark
Designer: Sara Radka
Fact Checkers: Ann Schwab & Eleanor Cardell

Photo Credits
Flickr: Aaron Parecki, 36, Jonathan Elliot, 5, 39, SimsTime, 20; Getty Images: Christian Petersen, 25, Dan R. Krauss, 3, Daniel Zuchnik, 30, Sascha Steinbach, 35; Newscom: Frances M. Roberts, 13, Max Dolberg/ZUMA Press, 7, WENN, 42, Pixabay: Clker-Free-Vector-Images, 4, VOLLEX, 5; Shutterstock: madamF, cover, 1, Merrell Made, 4, pil76, 9, 10, Teerawit Chankowet, 29, Vera Aksionava, 16

Library of Congress Cataloging-in-Publication Data
Names: Bolte, Mari, author.
Title: The sims / by Mari Bolte.
Description: Chicago : Norwood House Press, 2022. | Series: A great game! |
   Includes index. | Audience: Ages 8-10 | Audience: Grades 4-6 |
Summary: "An introductory look at the game of The SIMS. Describes the history of the game, introduces the
   creators and innovators, highlights competitions, and provides insight about the game's future. Informational
   text for readers who are new to The SIMS, or are interested in learning more. Includes a glossary, index, and
   bibliography for further reading. Explores the video game franchise The Sims, a virtual world where players
   can play at life by getting a job, making friends, and building a dream home"-- Provided by publisher.
Identifiers: LCCN 2021049731 (print) | LCCN 2021049732 (ebook) | ISBN 9781684507917
   (hardcover) | ISBN 9781684047277 (paperback) | ISBN 9781684047314 (epub)
Subjects: LCSH: Sims (Video game)--Juvenile literature.
Classification: LCC GV1469.35.S56 B65 2022 (print) | LCC GV1469.35.S56 (ebook) | DDC 794.8--dc23/eng/20211109
LC record available at https://lccn.loc.gov/2021049731
LC ebook record available at https://lccn.loc.gov/2021049732

Hardcover ISBN: 978-1-68450-791-7
Paperback ISBN: 978-1-68404-727-7

The Sims™ is a registered trademark of Electronic Arts, Inc.
This book is not associated with The Sims™, Electronic Arts, or any of its associated partners.

347N—012022
Manufactured in the United States of America in North Mankato, Minnesota.

Table of Contents

Shoo Flee!

You just got home from work. It has been a long day. You are hungry and tired. A quick rest on the couch will help regain some energy.

Suddenly, the doorbell rings. It's your neighbor, Mortimer Goth. He is dressed in a fancy suit. He asks about your day. You are too tired to talk to him and ask him to leave.

A Sim reacting to events or interactions on its own, such as smelly trash or a fire, is called autonomous.

You head to the kitchen to make yourself some food. Suddenly, mid-meal, your stove catches on fire! You panic! "Shoo flee!" you yell. This means, "There's a problem!" Will your brand-new house burn down? This is just another day in the life of The Sims.

History of The Sims

Will Wright wanted to be an astronaut. He studied robotics. He tried computer programming. In 1984, he made a game called Raid on Bungeling Bay. It was an action game. Players flew a helicopter and blew up factories. Raid on Bungeling Bay sold about a million copies on the Nintendo Entertainment System, mostly in Japan. Blowing stuff up was fun. But Wright found that he would rather build things instead. His next game was called SimCity.

In 1987, Wright met Jeff Braun at a party. Braun was a businessman. He wanted to get into making video games. Braun sold his company, and Wright had some money from Raid on Bungeling Bay. The two paired up. They started Maxis Software.

DID YOU KNOW?

Wright tried to sell SimCity to Broderbund, the company that published Raid on Bungeling Bay. They turned it down. They wanted games with a beginning and an end.

Will Wright left Maxis in 2009. In 2021, he put out a call for creators to help him with a new **simulation** game called Proxi.

SimCity was released in February 1989. The game quickly grew in popularity. *The New York Times* wrote about it. *Time* and *Newsweek* did full-page reviews. It was the first time they had written a computer game review. By 1992, more than a million copies had been sold.

In 1991, Wright lost his house and car to wildfires. It made him think about things that matter most in life: relationships. Buying new things to replace what was lost made him wonder why people bought things to make them happy. He started making a game with the idea of building and living a life.

A game about going to work, doing chores, and saying hello to your neighbors was hard to sell. All the board of directors at Maxis saw was an **interactive** dollhouse. Other games let players fight a war or play football or rescue a princess. They didn't think those players would want to do tasks like taking out the trash or cleaning the toilet. People at Maxis started calling it "the toilet game."

DID YOU KNOW?

Maxis made sequels to SimCity, including SimEarth and SimAnt. SimAnt put players in charge of an ant colony. At times, the ants seemed smarter than the game's huge, clumsy humans. It got Wright thinking about the future of **artificial intelligence**.

SimCity is an open-ended video game. Open-ended games allow the player to build and explore at whatever pace they like.

History of The Sims: Time Line

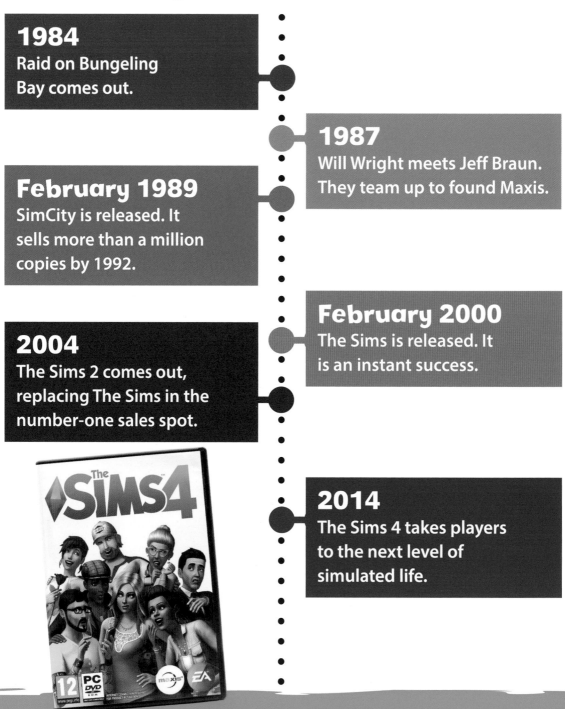

1984
Raid on Bungeling Bay comes out.

1987
Will Wright meets Jeff Braun. They team up to found Maxis.

February 1989
SimCity is released. It sells more than a million copies by 1992.

February 2000
The Sims is released. It is an instant success.

2004
The Sims 2 comes out, replacing The Sims in the number-one sales spot.

2014
The Sims 4 takes players to the next level of simulated life.

In 1997, Electronic Arts (EA) bought Maxis. They gave Wright's "toilet game" a chance. They gave Wright the team he needed to finish The Sims. It premiered at the 1999 Electronics Entertainment Expo (E3). Like SimCity before it, The Sims did not get a lot of attention—at first. But soon, people started talking. Players got excited to see what it was about. It turns out that players love doing chores—as long as their Sim is doing it for them!

The Sims came out in February 2000. It sold 11 million copies in the first two years. It would be the best-selling PC game for the next four years. In 2004, it lost the number-one spot. The game that replaced it was The Sims 2.

Speaking Simlish

Having characters talk to each other was important to Wright. But speaking English would get boring because there were only so many responses that they could pre-record. The first idea was to have them speak a lesser-known language, like Navajo, Estonian, or Ukrainian. But voice actors struggled with the unfamiliar words. The actors tried playing an improv game where they had to communicate by using made-up words. The game led to the creation of a whole Sim language called Simlish.

Expansion packs add interest to the original game. Livin' Large was the first expansion pack. It came out in August 2000. Six more expansion packs followed. Each expansion pack added new items, jobs, scenarios, and locations.

The Sims 2 came out in 2004. It had a fully **3D** world. In the game, Sims experienced aging and life stages. The Sims 2 had eight expansion packs and nine stuff packs. Stuff packs added new furniture, clothing, and decorations.

The Sims 3 was released in 2009. The Sim characters had even more personality, with wishes and goals. Eleven expansion packs and nine stuff packs were added later. Sims could make a movie, visit an island paradise, go to college, and see the future.

In 2014, The Sims 4 took players to the next level of Sim life. They could fully customize their Sims. Sims could explore new neighborhoods and worlds. When the game launched, there were five different editions. Each had its own set of exclusive items and things that made it unique. So far, 11 expansion packs have been released.

DID YOU KNOW?

The currency in The Sims and SimCity is called Simoleons. The Simoleon symbol is §. Simoleons are not based on any actual real money. Other in-game forms of currency are Lifestyle Points and Social Points. Social Points can be purchased by spending real money or can be earned in-game.

The Sims Online came out in 2002. It encouraged players to work together to learn new skills.

The Sims Basics

Step into the world of The Sims with a Sim character that's completely you. For new players, there's a tutorial version. Fewer customizable options mean jumping into the game faster. There is also a story mode. This chooses the Sim's look based on the questions the player answers.

For players who have the time or experience, there's Create-A-Sim. There are more than 700 different accessories to choose from.

Choosing the Sim's personality is next. Up to three **traits** can be chosen from the Social, Emotional, Lifestyle, and Hobby traits menus. The traits affect the way the Sim thinks and acts. Active Sims won't like being inside all the time. Materialistic Sims like to buy new things.

A Sim's **aspiration** sets that Sim's goal for the rest of its life. There are many different aspirations to choose from. Some Sims might like to learn new things. Others want to make a lot of friends.

DID YOU KNOW?

Sims age as the game is played. Players can get more time out of their Sim if they start life as a Young Adult. The game settings can also be changed to slow aging. Sims can also drink a potion or earn a Long Lived trait to stay young.

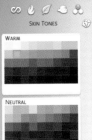

Endless options mean every Sim can look different. Sims can be any age from babies to adults. Walk style, physical frame, voice tone, and facial features give Sims originality.

Knock, knock! It's your new roommate! Will you get along?

Your Sim is built. Now it needs a place to live! Tutorial mode puts Sims in an already-built home with a roommate. Pop-up windows guide new players and teach them how to control their Sim and make it happy.

Making friends, getting a job, and earning money are essential Sim care. Health bars showing Bladder, Hunger, Energy, Fun, Social, and Hygiene need to be watched to make sure the Sim stays happy. If any of those bars get low, the Sim's mood will get worse. It will be harder to get them to cooperate and do tasks. If the Hunger bar runs out, the Sim will eventually die.

Similar Simulations

Without the success of SimCity and The Sims, many simulation games would not exist today. Once players figured out it was fun to do everyday tasks in a video game, other companies decided to copy the idea. Animal Crossing, Harvest Moon, Second Life, Farmville, Stardew Valley, and Minecraft are all examples of life simulation games. Paralives builds on what makes The Sims so popular and will take it to the next level. Cities: Skylines goes all the way back to SimCity's origins and gives players the chance to build and maintain a city.

At the beginning of the game, players start with 20,000 Simoleons. They must buy land and build a home. Every single part of the house costs money to build. A first home must be modest and practical. Houses are measured by tiled squares on a grid. Tools help the player start with basic building.

The most basic things a Sim needs are a place to rest, a place to make food and eat, and a bathroom. Then they need items to help them with their job, and things to keep them entertained.

Cheats and Codes

There are ways to cheat at the game. The original version let players use the codes "rosebud" and "klapaucius" to earn instant cash. The other **franchise** games have continued this tradition.

On a PC, players just need to press Ctrl + Shift + C and a cheat box will pop up. By entering different cheat codes, players can find themselves instantly rewarded. "TestingCheats" opens up a huge number of play cheats, from setting all a Sim's health bars to full, adding a Sim to a family, moving a Sim quickly, or gaining an infinite amount of money.

Homes can be built in interesting shapes and with different levels. Creators can give their homes a certain mood or feel, or even make them haunted.

Cancel (Esc)

The Sims 4 expansion pack, Get Famous, let Sims become celebrities, earn awards, complete gigs, meet fans, and become investors.

Sims have bills that pile up. Choosing a high-paying job that is also exciting and rewarding is important. This is true in the game and in real life!

There are a few ways a Sim can earn money. The most obvious way is to get a job. Sims go to work during the week and get paid. Sims that leave for work in good moods and complete daily tasks earn promotions. Promotions also come after learning new skills.

What do you want to do when you grow up? Sims have a lot of choices! Is your Sim a star? Join a talent agency and book some gigs. Maybe they would rather see the stars as an astronaut! Sports, business, city or park planning, and jobs in the food industry are a few other choices. Sims can even choose to live a life of crime or be a crime fighter.

Expansion packs add even more job options. New choices include influencers, writers, scientists, secret agents, and gardeners.

DID YOU KNOW?

The highest-paid career in The Sims 4 is an Interstellar Smuggler. Sims in this line of work make 413 Simoleons an hour. Sims with this job move goods across the galaxy. It's a dangerous line of work, but someone has to do it!

Every time two characters meet, they gain or lose relationship points. Close friends and family members like being around each other. They will want to spend more time together. More casual friends might dislike each other. They might even fight.

Time and effort must be spent on relationships to make them work. Points will be lost if a friend isn't invited over. And if a Sim is in a bad mood, hanging out will be even harder. Nobody likes spending time with a grump! Each Sim is different too. Players must learn how to talk to each friend, neighbor, and coworker. Likes, dislikes, and moods vary. Saying or doing the wrong thing might lose points for the player.

Dating, getting married, and starting families is the next step. Health bars for Friendship and Romance help Sims make friends. Friends and partners can help boost a player's Fun, Hunger, and Social health bars. This can lead to promotions at work or extra spending money. It can even save a Sim from an early death!

DID YOU KNOW?

Sims with relationships of 80 or higher can become best friends. The option to ask them to be best friends will pop up. Sims can only have one best friend at a time.

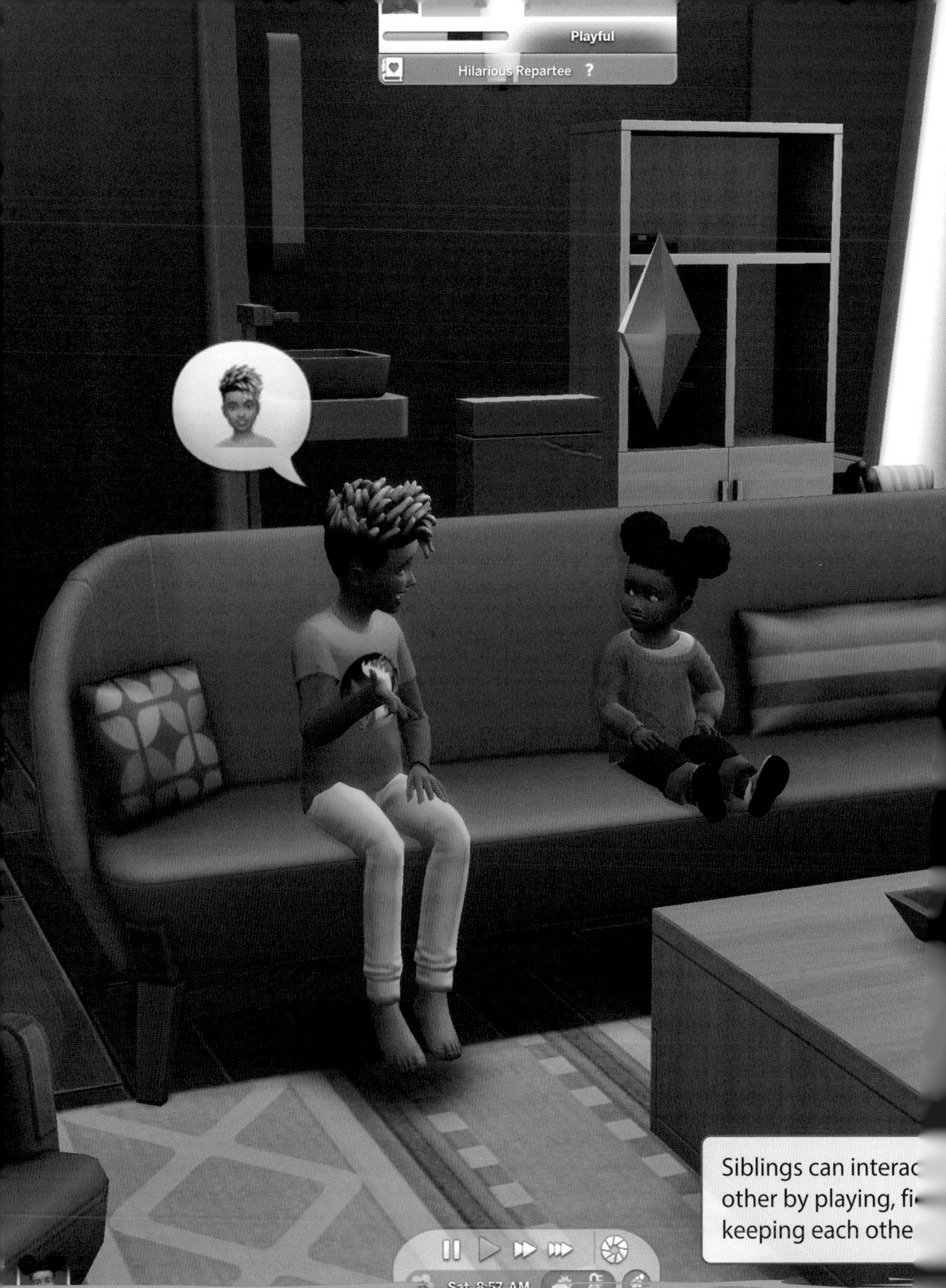

Siblings can interac
other by playing, fi
keeping each othe

The Sims Community

The Sims gives players many ways to show off what they've made. Online galleries, forums, and social media accounts are all places to share. Websites think up community challenges with themes or rules. The challenges let creators try new techniques or styles they haven't used before. Challenges are open to any player, any age, anywhere.

EA hosts an online gallery. Users can upload their own home, room, and character designs. Other gamers can "favorite" things in the gallery. They can then download them for their own use. The top picks are shown right on the website's front page. A browse tab helps players find new additions to their own game.

DID YOU KNOW?

More than 30 million unique players around the world have logged on to The Sims 4. By 2019, The Sims franchise had made more than $5 billion in revenue. In total, 200 million copies of The Sims games have been sold on PC.

EA's Play event first introduced fans to the Island Living expansion pack in 2019.

Custom content creators give characters, homes, and accessories a fresh update.

ALLERY | NEWS | | MY LIBRARY

Search everyone's creations!

Item Name | Enter Item Name

FAMILIE

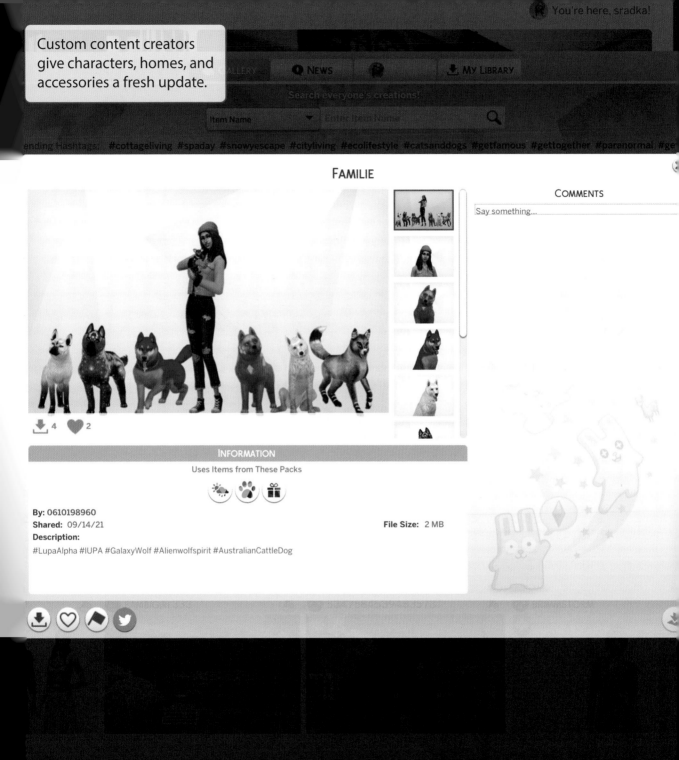

COMMENTS

Say something...

4   2

INFORMATION

Uses Items from These Packs

By: 0610198960
Shared: 09/14/21
File Size: 2 MB
Description:
#LupaAlpha #IUPA #GalaxyWolf #Alienwolfspirit #AustralianCattleDog

Custom content creators take DIY to the next level. Custom content (CC) is any game content not made by EA. It adds **textures** to the game's graphics. There are two types—Maxis Match (MM) and Alpha. Maxis Match is similar to the graphics found in the game. Alpha is anything that falls outside the game's style.

Some CC creators have been playing The Sims for years. They have a huge following. Advanced levels of design detail, high fashion, new colors and patterns, and lots of updates are ways to get noticed as a CC creator. There are many mods of older versions of The Sims too.

Simlish Soap Operas

Drama mods give players more interesting, dramatic, or realistic storylines. They might change the way Sims react emotionally to each other. In the regular game, a Sim can experience happiness and then sadness instantly. The longer a Sim stays angry or sad, the more work it will take to make them happy. In a regular game, Sims can be a little mean or a little unlikeable, but a mod can make them really hard to like. A mod that forces the player to work through a Sim's emotions gives the player a deeper connection to the game.

EA has tried out online and interactive gameplay before. The Sims Online was a massively multiplayer online game (MMO). It came out in 2002. For $9.99 a month, players could gather in 12 different cities. They could learn new skills. Items could be bought and sold. But EA eventually stopped supporting the site. It was renamed EA Land in 2007, but did not do well. Finally, it was shut down in 2008.

The Sims Bustin' Out came out in 2003. Players on the Playstation 2 had an online play option. They could send their Sim on a weekend getaway with up to 30 people.

The Sims Social was a version for Facebook. EA hoped people would play online and invite their Facebook friends. Due to lack of interest, though, The Sims Social and other EA Sims games were shut down.

The Sims FreePlay first came out for mobile devices in 2011. Simmers could complete quests in real time while on the go.

Sims Mobile was released for iOS and Android on March 6, 2018. It is based on The Sims 4. It also lets players visit and connect with real-life friends.

DID YOU KNOW?

The Sims 4 has no official multiplayer mode. However, there is a mod that makes it possible. One player's computer acts as a **server**. Up to 12 other players can join the game.

If your Sim has a deep enough romantic relationship with another Sim, your Sim can propose!

At one point, The Sims Mobile was the third-most downloaded game in the Apple App store.

Millie Bobby Brown plays The Sims because of the creativity and diversity the game offers.

Watching someone play The Sims on Twitch or YouTube is called Let's Play. The player talks to the audience as they play, telling jokes or adding comments. Most of the top Sim streamers are female. Many keep it family-friendly. Commenters are expected to be nice to each other.

Some streamers use Let's Play for challenges. Watching the streamer's progress gives viewers a reason to tune in day after day. Other Let's Plays tell a story. The streamer might give each Sim a different voice and act out a web series. Let's Plays also give ideas to other players. Build tips or design themes keep watchers interested.

Some Simmers have star power already. In 2018, Millie Bobby Brown was chosen as a Sims Ambassador. A Sim version of Brown was made available in the EA Gallery. Her Sim also was the Event Coordinator for the Positivity Challenge. The Positivity Challenge encourages Sims to do nice things for other Sims. Players were rewarded with gifts to use in the game.

DID YOU KNOW?

Past Sims Ambassadors include Vanessa Hudgens, HWASA, Bilal Hassani, and GOT7 member BamBam. Some were part of the company's Play With Life campaign, and their Sims can still be downloaded.

In 2020, EA started Stay Home, Play Together. It asked people to stay home but play together as COVID-19 swept the globe. In April, a week of Sim-specific Twitch **streaming** took place. Streamers from around the world got together online to tell a story in The Sims. The event was called The House Party.

The first streamer built the location for the story. The next created characters. Finally, the next three streamers told the story. People watching gave suggestions over live chat. Their ideas influenced the storytellers. Codes for free items were given out. Fans were encouraged to follow #SimTogether on Twitter.

E-Sports

Playing e-sports is an after-school activity that a Sim can participate in. Becoming one is the same as getting a job. And, like any job, completing daily tasks and building skills are essential to moving up in the e-sports world. Charisma and video game skills are the most important skills to build. At the highest level, a Sim can even earn a sponsorship as a bonus. Then, by choosing the Tech Guru career, a Sim can turn gaming into an actual job.

During Stay Home, Play Together, EA partnered with the NFL, NBA, NHL, FIFA, and UFC to encourage gamers to connect online.

LEVEL UP

MONICA HAS REACHED LEVEL 2 OF THE COOKING SKILL!

The Future of The Sims

The Sims celebrated its 20-year anniversary in 2020. Fans shared their favorite Sim moments, fan art, costumes, and recipes. Expansion and stuff packs were given away. Fans could also buy special Sims shirts online.

Although the game has stayed true to its roots, its more than 75 expansion and stuff packs have let the world grow in a huge way. More than 30 million unique players around the world have created a Sim. In 2020 alone, Sims had around 10 million active users.

To Another 20 Years

When The Sims turned 20, EA released some exciting Sims stats about the game.

- more than 1.6 billion Sims created
- 6.9 million vampires
- 1 million mermaids
- 575 million Sim households built
- 65 million hours spent searching the Gallery
- 41 million uploads
- 825 million downloads

The Create-a-Sim demo was a popular stop at Gamescom, a gaming trade show.

Sims fans watch streamers take on challenges, make home improvements, show off mods, or even show off how fast they can create a new character.

People like playing The Sims. They like watching other people play The Sims. So why wouldn't they like watching a reality show about people playing The Sims? *The Sims Spark'd* was a web contest reality show. Episodes aired on TBS and Buzzfeed Multiplayer's YouTube channel. The first episode was released online on July 20, 2020.

Twelve popular Simmers competed for a $100,000 prize. They were split into three-person groups. There was a Stylist, a Builder, and a Storyteller. In-game challenges tested their creativity. Each week, one team was eliminated.

The fourth and final episode aired on August 10, 2020. Team Llama won the last challenge. They created a story about female gamers being bullied.

Realistic Skins

Xmiramira, a Black Simmer, was part of the *Spark'd Challenge* winning team. Xmiramira noticed that she couldn't make Sims that represented her in her Let's Plays. Although there was a darker-skinned option, the tone looked gray or purple. There were no mods to fix the problem. So she took on the challenge herself. Her Melanin Packs add dozens of skin tones and makeup options. After Xmiramira's win, EA announced they would add more hairstyles and skin tones later in the year.

EA has found ways to keep the game fresh for fans! Kitchen gadgets, new fashions, furry pets, and cool technology can be added thanks to expansion packs. In July 2021, the latest expansion pack, Cottage Living, was released. Players got a new world inspired by England. Farm animals like llamas, cows, and bunnies live together. Sims can garden and grow their own food. A weekly farm fest lets all the Sims come together to show off their crops.

New expansion packs mean new cheats, too. Cottage Living has its own cheat codes. The ability to befriend all the animals on the farm, get all available recipes for animal feed and treats, and buy animal clothes are some of them.

The Cottage Living expansion pack challenges players to find ingredients to cook meals. They have to defeat a sneaky fox. Can they live off the grid? Off-the-grid has appeared in other expansion packs, too, like Island Living. It encourages Sims to make money in unusual ways. They must raise their own food or earn money outside a typical job.

DID YOU KNOW?

Fans of The Sims love to build their favorite scenes and locations! Movie and Broadway play sets, vacation sites, and real-life real estate properties are some of the more creative uses of the game.

The Cool Kitchen expansion pack gave Simmers many new things for their home—including an ice cream maker that could make any flavor imaginable.

Building tiny or minimalist homes was already a popular idea before Tiny Living came out. The stuff pack gave players more ways to add details to their homes.

People are always thinking up new and interesting ways to get into the world of The Sims. One streamer, DrGluon, combined The Sims with his other favorite simulation game, Stardew Valley. In Stardrew Valley, players build farms and raise animals. DrGluon used Cottage Living to copy his 2D Stardew Valley farm and town into the 3D world of The Sims. Every house, path, and even every tree is in the same place. The Stardew Valley characters are all Sims, too.

In January 2020, The Sims Tiny Living Stuff Pack came out. Ahead of its release, EA put out a Tiny Living challenge. Could Simmers create a tiny house that fits on a 20-by-15 tiled lot? The house needed to be practical and functional, but small and original. Ten winners got a free copy of the stuff pack.

DID YOU KNOW?

There are many kinds of challenges for Simmers online.
Many are based on those found on reality TV shows
like Big Brother, The Bachelor, and MasterChef.

Pets was the fourth expansion pack for The Sims 2. EA launched the game by inviting a pet stylist to the stars in Los Angeles, California, to come play.

There have been 11 expansion packs, 10 game packs, 18 stuff packs, and 4 kits for The Sims 4. All have given players new items and options. Expansion packs are the biggest in-game boost. But the other packs offer plenty of new content.

Game packs add more skills and abilities. Sometimes they add new places to visit or live. They let players live in fantasy worlds.

Stuff packs are full of outfits, hairstyles, skills, and decorations. Crafts, hobbies, and other interests can be explored.

Kits are mini collections. They contain throwback wardrobes, country kitchen appliances, housecleaning items, and a Moroccan-themed patio set.

Whether you're an experienced Simmer or just starting out, there are always plenty of ways to stay busy in the world of The Sims! Create, build, and grow your Sims to give them the most interesting Sim life possible.

Expansion Packs (in order of release)

- Get to Work
- Get Together
- City Living
- Cats and Dogs
- Seasons
- Get Famous
- Island Living
- Discover University
- Eco Lifestyle
- Snowy Escape
- Cottage Living

Glossary

3D: three dimensional

artificial intelligence: a computer that can simulate human intelligence or emotion

aspiration: a hope or ambition of achieving something

expansion: a thing that broadens a world

franchise: a group, such as teams, games, or movies, that are about the same characters or take place in the same world

interactive: two things communicating with each other

server: a computer or computer program that acts as a centralized resource

simulation: a computer model of something

streaming: any media content, live or recorded, that is delivered to computers and mobile devices over the internet

textures: the feel, appearance, or consistency of surfaces

traits: distinguishing qualities or characteristics about a person

For More Information

Books

Wainewright, Max. *Scratch Code Smart Homes*. New York: Crabtree Publishing, 2020.

Woodcock, Jon. *Coding Projects in Scratch*. New York: DK Publishing, 2019.

Websites

Code Tutorials (https://code.org/learn) One-hour coding tutorials for people of all ages.

Electronic Arts (https://www.ea.com/games/the-sims) The official Electronic Arts website for The Sims, with news, downloads, and game challenges.

Index

About the Author

Mari Bolte has worked in publishing as a writer and editor for more than 15 years. She has written dozens of books about things like science and craft projects, historical figures and events, and pop culture. She lives in Minnesota.